S0-BCK-426

SUMMARY
of
10% HAPPIER

*A FastReads Summary with
Key Takeaways & Analysis*

NOTE: The purpose of this FastReads summary is to help you decide if it's worth the time, money and effort reading the original book (if you haven't already). FastReads has pulled out the essence with commentary and critique—but only to help you ascertain the value of the book for yourself. This summary is meant to be a supplement to, and not a replacement for *10% Happier*.

Copyright © 2017 by FastReads. All rights reserved. This book or parts thereof may not be reproduced in any form, stored in any retrieval system, or transmitted in any form by any means—electronic, mechanical, photocopy, recording, or otherwise—without prior written permission of the publisher, except as provided by United States of America copyright law. This is an unofficial summary for educational purposes and is not intended as a substitute or replacement for the original book.

TABLE OF CONTENTS

EXECUTIVE SUMMARY

In this acclaimed memoir, Dan Harris recounts the events leading to his televised panic attack and takes the reader through the subsequent quest to find himself. In an accidental journey involving evangelicals, self-help gurus, Buddhists, and neuroscientists, Harris narrates how he discovered he had been sleepwalking his entire life. He paints a vibrant picture of mindless living as he reveals his pursuit of the thrill of war reporting and his indulgence in hard drugs.

Harris recounts how he discovered his internal monologue was at the root of his mindless behavior and how an unlikely practice gave him a way out. He narrates how he learned meditation, nurtured compassion in an aggressive industry, and found lasting happiness. He sets out to demystify meditation and show it can work for anyone. In his view, you don't have to lose your edge, creativity, or success habits when you quiet the incessant voice in your head.

CHAPTER 1: AIR HUNGER

On June 7, 2004, Harris was on the set of *Good Morning America* filling in for another news reader when a wave of panic hit him halfway through his live voice-overs. About five million people tuned to ABC News watched as he stammered and lost his voice. He had been with the network for four years. In his view, an extended period of mindlessness coupled with blind ambition had led to this moment.

Before Harris got to ABC News, he had worked with local news for seven years. Fresh out of college, he had taken a part-time job paying minimum wage at the NBC station in Bangor, Maine. The producer assigned to him once remarked that the job was not a glamorous one, but Harris loved it all the same. Although he dreamed of working with a major news network, he figured that it wouldn't happen until he was about forty years old.

Months into his job with the NBC station, Harris convinced his bosses to put him on camera. He was barely twenty-two when the station made him a reporter and anchor. Not long afterwards, he moved to larger markets and found bigger stories and better pay. He was working at a cable news channel in Boston when his agent informed him that ABC executives were interested in him.

The network hired him as the co-anchor of *World News Now* – an overnight newscast that aired from two to four in the morning. Since the anchor he was replacing had decided to stay with the network, Harris was asked to file stories for the weekend edition of the network's evening newscast, World News Tonight. The job gave him a chance to broadcast to millions of people across the country. For the next five years, Harris was a news correspondent with his idol, Peter Jennings, as his mentor.

Eventually, Harris got over the incredulity of the network hiring him and started focusing on making the most out of the opportunity. Since his childhood, he had strived to strike a balance between hyper vigilance and contentment. He lost sight of this balance as soon as ABC hired him. He worked three times as hard as his peers to prove himself – constantly pitching stories and often skipping social important events to be on air.

Following the 9/11 attacks, the network sent Harris to Pakistan. Harris, who had missed the chance to report on what would probably be the biggest story of his career (the 9/11 attacks), was ecstatic. Shortly after landing in Pakistan in October, the Taliban invited the ABC News crew to its home base in Kandahar. The crew drove through the aftermath of U.S air bombings and socialized with child soldiers. Harris, who had never been to a third world country, did not realize how unprepared he was for the psychological consequences that came with the experience. He was already hooked to the danger and publicity that came with conflict reporting.

Fueled by the desire to be part of big stories, Harris spent the next three years travelling from ABC's offices in New York to places like Iraq, Israel, and Gaza. His indifferent attitude to the horrors he witnessed was surprising, even for him. While his parents worried about the trauma war correspondents experience, he thrived in the chaos, the joy of being chauffeured like a head of state, and the sense of purpose that came with reporting pivotal historical events.

The overly competitive culture of the network meant that Harris had to fight for airtime with his colleagues. When he was not traversing conflict zones with his crew, he was constantly lobbying the anchors and executives who made the reporting assignments. The intensity of his work not only stressed him, but also pressed him to measure himself against his colleagues. Consequently, he resented the correspondents who were more successful than he was.

When Harris returned to New York in 2003, he realized that the small social network had had formed when he was a domestic reporter had withered away. Most of his friends had families now but – even in his early thirties – settling down was not among his priorities. Not long after he got home, he developed flulike symptoms that persisted for months. A psychiatrist diagnosed him with depression. The psychiatrist speculated that either war reporting had traumatized him or he was suffering withdrawal from his addiction to the thrill of his past assignments.

While Harris had never experimented with hard drugs before, the dejected feeling that came with depression was pushing him to try anything that would restore a sense of normalcy. When a friend offered him cocaine at a party, he was almost happy to partake. He discovered the euphoric energy that came with the drug and, not long afterwards, the bliss that came with ecstasy. But the end of the high came with a deep emptiness. He limited his substance abuse to weekends to prevent hangovers from interfering with his work.

Despite the professional risk he knew he was taking, Harris continued taking cocaine to abate his depression symptoms. He hit rock bottom on the morning he suffered a panic attack on the set of Good Morning America. His lungs felt like they were caving in and he experienced what doctors call "air hunger." He never admitted to suffering a panic attack. He feared his colleagues would label him a fraud.

After the panic attack, Harris' mother set him up with a psychiatrist who prescribed antianxiety medication. He continued partying and suffered another panic attack on set not long afterwards. Luckily, no one seemed to have noticed it. His parents found him a new psychiatrist who informed him that cocaine use exacerbated the risk of panic attacks. He advised Harris to quit cocaine and take better care of himself.

The biweekly sessions Harris had with the psychiatrist made him realize how his mindless behavior had pushed him to care little for anything other than airtime, to traverse war zones without regard for psychological consequences, and to risk everything he had worked for with his drug addiction.

CHAPTER 2: UNCHURCHED

After the 2004 elections, Harris resumed the religious assignment Peter Jennings had given him years before. Following the pivotal role evangelicals had played in the re-election of George W. Bush, Harris would traverse the country reporting on major religious events and public arguments over gay marriage, abortion, and the role of religion in the public space. Amidst all of this religious coverage, he remained disinterested in matters of faith. He had grown up in a secular environment and his parents had let him know – when he was only nine years old – that there was no God.

Harris was in pursuit of another cultural war when he wound up at the New Life mega church in Colorado Springs. The church, which Pastor Ted Haggard had founded a decade earlier, had fourteen thousand members and was home to a number of Christian organizations. At the end of the interview with Ted, the pastor asked to talk to Harris off the record. Harris, who was reluctant to take up the offer, marveled at the fact that the pastor did not try to convert him or make him feel "unchurched." The encounter made him realize just how much he had blindly bought into religious stereotypes. Religious people, he realized, were not unintelligent, poor, or easy to command.

After Peter Jennings succumbed to lung cancer, the network made several reshuffles and moved Harris to the Sunday edition of World News. He prided himself in the fact that this promotion allowed him to pick the stories to cover and deliver them on the chair that Jennings once occupied. The only thing that did not change in the network was the incessant rivalry for airtime. The resentment that Harris harbored for correspondents who beat him to vital stories only intensified.

Throughout this period, it never crossed Harris' mind that he could find answers to his personal struggles in the religious traditions he covered. All the same, he continued with his plan to shed more light – rather than heat – on religious happenings. He profiled Mormon apostles, interviewed born-again Christians, and even covered atheist conventions. Ted Haggard became his reference whenever he needed answers on evangelicalism.

It took Harris by surprise when, on one November morning in 2006, he learned that Ted led a double life. A male escort, who had reached out to the network's affiliate in Denver, claimed that he had a sexual relationship with the pastor. The escort also divulged that he supplied the pastor with drugs and had voice recordings to prove it. Days later, Ted, who had initially refuted the allegations, confessed that he had a dark side and resigned from his evangelical positions.

Weeks after Ted's debacle, an office colleague set Harris up on a date with a doctor friend. Harris, who was initially skeptical about the matchmaking, was immediately stricken by Bianca's beauty, humility, and optimism. She moved into his apartment three months after their first date. Harris found it strangely pleasurable to be in love for the first time in his life. He delighted in the fact that she made him a better person.

Nearly a year after Ted admitted to living a double life (and subsequently disappearing from public life) he reached out to Harris and accepted to do a follow-up interview. From being named by Time Magazine the 11th most influential American evangelical a year before, Ted was now selling insurance and living in a low-key apartment in Arizona. He told Harris that he was heterosexual, not gay, and that it was the culture of hatefulness in the modern church that forced him to live a lie. He confessed that for the year or so he had been in hiding, he had actively contemplated suicide. Only his faith had held him back.

Harris likened his own challenges to those of Ted. He envied Ted for his firm belief that his troubles were part of a larger plan. Ted helped him appreciate the value of having a purpose that transcended the demands of daily responsibilities.

CHAPTER 3: GENIUS OR LUNATIC?

Three years after his panic attack, Harris had gone off his antianxiety medication and was, by all measures, faring well. He was only seeing his psychiatrist about once in a month and had managed to hold off his drug cravings. At the same time, he was planning a wedding with Bianca. Although he was successfully anchoring the Sunday edition of World News and had been tasked with launching major investigations for Nightline, his worries about work were intensifying. He worried about the unpredictability of his job and grew anxious over the thought that his receding hairline would cost him his career.

At one time, Harris was out in Jersey City doing a piece on the beliefs of Pentecostals. The crew producer mentioned that she had recently read a book about controlling ego by Eckhart Tolle. She told Harris the author would make for a good story. Harris ordered the book (*A New Earth: Awakening to Your Life's Purpose*) when he got home and received it a few days later.

Although Harris was initially put off by Tolle's stately writing style and the grandiosity of its marketing content, he was fascinated by the book's thesis. The author asserted that an incessant self-referential voice governs people all their lives. The voice, which is mostly negative, judges and labels everything it encounters – both within and without. Tolle underscored ego as the sense of "I" and asserted that most people take it for granted, the consequence of which is mindless living followed by undesirable consequences. Harris recognized that the voice in his head had led him to do cocaine and pursue the thrill of conflict reporting.

Harris realized that the book's depiction of ego encapsulated his entire life's behavior. Tolle's contention that ego is never satisfied made Harris realize why he could never get enough airtime and drugs. He also realized that his ego was always pushing him to measure his self-worth against everyone else.

"The ego is never satisfied. No matter how much stuff we buy, no matter how many arguments we win or delicious meals we consume, the ego never feels complete."

Harris also learned that ego thrives on drama, and that it dwells on the past and the future, rarely on the present. He understood why he always brought his office baggage home and why he was so good at avoiding the present. He realized he was always checking things off his to-do list, chasing deadlines, and fantasizing that whatever came next would be better. With these revelations, it dawned on Harris that he had been sleepwalking his entire life.

While Harris got the impression that Tolle wrote the book with him in mind, he couldn't help but wonder – thanks to some absurd claims – whether the author was a genius or a lunatic. He claimed, for example, that living in the present slowed the aging process. With some research, Harris realized Tolle struggled with suicidal thoughts as a graduate at Oxford University. At some point Tolle had a magical revelation; an overnight panacea so strong that he went on to live on park benches in a state of pure bliss. He moved to Canada afterwards to write the book.

Harris was reading Tolle's book when he discovered a small milky patch on his right cheek. His dermatologist informed him the patch was a nonlethal form of skin cancer and arranged for its removal. When he realized the incision would leave a scar, he immediately visualized the end of his career on T.V. Somehow, perhaps as a result of Tolle's wisdom, he realized this scenario would not necessarily play out and hushed his worrying voice. The dermatologist removed the patch with a few facial surgeries.

When Harris realized he was not among the correspondents chosen to cover the inauguration of President Barack Obama, he could hardly contain his displeasure. He realized Tolle had made an elaborate diagnosis of ego and mindless behavior but had not offered any practical advice for real-life situations. While he agreed with Tolle's assertion that the future was a mental phantom, he figured he had to prepare for it to stay afloat in his competitive industry. He decided he had to meet Tolle.

Tolle agreed to a one-hour interview with Harris in Toronto where he was giving a sold-out speech. Harris prodded him for practical ways to stop the voice in his head. Tolle asserted that to do so, he had to take a conscious breath and observe his pattern of thoughts. Harris doubted the honesty of Tolle's answers when he proclaimed that he never experienced bad moods or harbored negative thoughts. All the same, he agreed with Tolle when he said one had to embrace the present and avoid treating it as an obstacle to a bigger moment in the future.

Key Takeaways

• An incessant stream of repetitive thinking – most of it negative – governs people their entire lives. The failure to recognize this voice pushes people to blindly act out their thoughts, often to undesirable results

• Ego focuses on the past and the future at the expense of the present. Lessen your focus on futuristic goals and enjoy the journey.

• Understand that everything negative happening now is what it is and avoid the temptation to personalize it.

CHAPTER 4: HAPPINESS, INC.

Harris met Deepak Chopra, another self-help guru, six weeks after his encounter with Tolle. He was moderating a Nightline debate on the topic of whether Satan exists and Chopra was one of the participants taking the "no" side. Before the debate, Harris took Chopra aside for a pre-interview. Chopra professed that he was permanently present – he did not regret the past or anticipate the present. He divulged that the trick was to separate oneself from the situation surrounding the moment.

The interview with Chopra attracted so much traffic that it ended up on the "most viewed" column of the ABC News website. Harris' boss, David Westin, called him in to talk about the weight of Chopra's ideas. Harris admitted he hadn't fully grasped the concept of living in the present and gave Westin a copy of Tolle's book to read instead.

Harris reached out to Chopra for concept clarification when he realized he couldn't convince anyone of the merit of living in the *Now*. Chopra, who had been sending copies of his books to Harris' office, invited him to the Manhattan outpost of the Chopra Center. The center offered medical consultations, spa treatments, yoga, and astrological readings.

Chopra had come a long way from being a depressed medical resident. After his residence, he had worked for the Maharishi Mahesh Yogi and later ventured out on his own. More recently, he had appeared on Forbes list of the richest celebrities

Harris found Chopra both interesting and incomprehensible, just like Tolle. He doubted Chopra's sincerity. For a man who claimed that he was never stressed, Chopra's body language often implied that he was on edge.

Not long after his encounter with Chopra, Harris and his producer decided to launch a series of stories covering the $11 billion self-help industry. They called it *Happiness Inc*. He interviewed leading figures like Joe Vitale, author of *The Secret*. He also interviewed other stars of the DVD version of the book and got the sense that their ideas on positive thinking were absurd and hypocritical. To say that the unconscious negative thoughts people harbored shaped their reality seemed like blaming the victims of natural disasters for their misfortunes.

Key Takeaways

• Living in the present means recognizing that everything happening – whether good or bad – will pass. It means separating oneself from the impermanent events surrounding each moment.

CHAPTER 5: THE JEW-BU

About eight months after he had discovered Tolle, Harris was in a hotel in downtown Manhattan to meet Dr. Mark Epstein. Epstein was a trained psychiatrist and practicing Buddhist. Bianca had given Harris a pair of books authored by Epstein which, she said, had helped her through difficult times in her twenties. As he read Epstein's books, Harris realized Tolle had taken Buddha's teachings on how the mind works and exaggerated them for profit.

Epstein affirmed that the inner voice is a childish protagonist who is constantly scheming and selfishly wanting more. He remarked that human beings had an innate tendency to jump from one experience to the next without achieving satisfaction – a tendency Harris quickly recognized in himself. Epstein asserted that one did not have to buy into Buddhist beliefs (about rebirth, karma and enlightenment) to benefit from the philosophy. He claimed Buddha was the original psychoanalyst and implied that adopting Buddhism was better than seeing a psychiatrist. While therapy offered an understanding of the human condition, it didn't offer the relief that Buddhism did.

Epstein made Harris realize why his psychiatrist could not do more than help him identify his mindless behavior, quit drugs, and stay on course. Determined to learn more, Harris bought several books on Buddhism. He realized that the main thesis of the philosophy was that people suffer because they hold on to things that don't last.

"The Buddha embraced an often overlooked truism: nothing lasts – including us. We and everyone we love will die. Fame fizzles, beauty fades, continents shift… we may know this intellectually, but on an emotional level we seem to be hardwired for denial."

The Buddha had argued some 2,500 years ago that true happiness could only come from understanding and embracing the constant state of impermanence in one's life. This understanding would enable one to distance themselves from the drama in their lives, see things in perspective, and let go.

While the Buddhist teachings put a lot of things in perspective for Harris, they left him with a lot of questions. He was concerned that letting go would lead to passivity, and that capping desire would undermine the will to strive. Nevertheless, he felt that the philosophy was giving him the sense of direction he craved.

Harris made a conscious note to put Buddha's teachings to use during his wedding weekend. He made deliberate efforts to pause, look around, and enjoy the little moments while they lasted. But back at work, his comparing and worrying mind was as alive as it ever was. With this realization, he reached out to Dr. Epstein and arranged a meeting.

Unlike the other self-help gurus Harris had met, Epstein admitted that he often felt sad, obsessive, and a range of other negative emotions. He admitted that while he tried to be in the present, he did not always succeed. He never had any sudden awakening, but Buddha's teachings had helped him overcome feelings of unreality and emptiness.

When Harris admitted that he only wanted to know how to manage his ego, Epstein recommended some beginner books he would find helpful. Harris was amused to note that almost all of the books Epstein recommended were authored by Jews. Epstein revealed that he had taken a religion class at Harvard with some of these authors. Years later, they had formed an Eastern spirituality subculture that they jokingly referred to as the Jew-Bus. Harris found the group legitimate and remarkable. But he found its teachings rather repellent.

Key Takeaways

• Buddha diagnosed the human condition more than 2,500 years ago and offered the relief that modern psychiatry struggles to provide.

• The failure to recognize the impermanence of things, experiences, and people is the root of human suffering.

• The inner voice is a selfish child who is constantly murmuring, scheming, and wanting more of everything. Most behavior is a reaction to the whims of this voice.

CHAPTER 6: THE POWER OF NEGATIVE THINKING

Epstein and other members of the Jew-Bus were making it clear that the only way to tame the restless inner voice was to meditate. Harris found the practice distasteful. Nevertheless, when his psychiatrist said meditation might be good for him, he picked up some Buddhist meditation books. He learned that meditation could lower blood pressure and reverse the effects of stress. He also learned that, contrary to his convictions, he did not need to wear robes or chant phrases to meditate.

Harris decided to try meditation while at a beach house with Bianca and some friends. The meditation book he was reading had simple instructions. All he had to do was sit comfortably, feel his breathing sensations, and gently refocus on breathing whenever his mind began to wander. He tried meditation for five minutes, all the while struggling to subdue the chatter in his mind. While he didn't really like the practice, he developed a new respect for it.

Harris tried meditating for ten minutes every day after his initial session. He found that trying to quiet his mind and focus on his breathing did not get easier with time. When his mind was not lost in random chatter, it was impatiently waiting for his alarm to go off. Still, he recognized that meditation offered a real remedy for his restless mind – something the likes of Tolle could not offer.

Harris found that focusing on his breath easily brought him to the present moment in situations where he had to wait or deal with something unpleasant. Meditation made him realize how the craving to be someone or somewhere else had filled his life.

Buddhism, Harris discovered, focused on mindfulness – the ability to recognize emotional states without being affected by them. Typically, people react to things they experience in three ways: they want them, reject them, or zone out. Mindfulness is another way to react to things one experiences. Mindfulness begins by making nonjudgmental notes of things like itches and avoiding the temptation to react. Mastering these simple things prepares one to master thoughts and emotions.

"The point of mindfulness was to short-circuit what had always been a habitual, mindless reaction."

Harris realized that the lack of this mindfulness had pushed him to replace drug cravings with food cravings. He also realized he could have used mindfulness to cope with the anxiety that came with the reshuffles at work.

Later on, Harris paid for and attended a Buddhist conference presided over by Mark Epstein. He brought along a friend who worried that he would lose his ability to write music if he became too happy. For his presentation, Epstein noted that mindfulness offered a way for people to examine their self-hatred without trying to make it go away. This examination liberates one's spirit in a way that buying things or suppressing emotions couldn't. Essentially, mindfulness made one more insightful, not less.

The next day, one of the co-speakers at the conference presented an effective method for applying mindfulness. She used a catchy acronym: RAIN.

R: Recognize – Pause and acknowledge your feelings.

A: Allow – Let your feelings be.

I: Investigate – Check how your feelings are physically affecting your body.

N: Non-identification – Understand that your feelings are passing states of mind.

Harris practiced the method a few weeks later when he worried that he would not get a promotion. As he anxiously lay on the couch, he noted the pounding in his head, the worry in his thoughts, and the buzzing in his chest. Not only did the investigation lessen the authority of the voice in his head, but it also gave him a sense of hope. However, he noted that while mindfulness eased his mental anguish, it did nothing to lessen his real-world problems.

Harris arranged another meeting with Epstein. Epstein explained that mindfulness allowed him to respond, rather than react, to his feelings. It would allow him to see a problem clearly and prevent him from acting blindly. He noted that while people cannot control what comes to mind, they can control how they handle their negative feelings. Mindfulness is a skill that improves as one meditates.

Epstein suggested that Harris should attend a meditation retreat organized by a teacher he revered – Joseph Goldstein. With the help of a friend, Harris signed up for the ten-day retreat in California.

Key Takeaways

• Traffic jams, confrontations, and others aspects of modern life often trigger the human body's fight-or flight mechanism and contribute to the development of heart diseases. Meditation can alleviate the effects of stress and lower blood pressure.

• To mediate, sit comfortably with your back upright and focus on your breathing. Gently bring your mind to your breathing when it begins to wander.

• Mindfulness tames the inner voice and lessens the tendency to blindly react to impulses and urges.

CHAPTER 7: RETREAT

Day One

Harris was acutely aware of the dread filling his mind as he prepared to check in at the meditation center. The informational materials distributed by the retreat center said there would be no communication with other members or the outside world. It would be ten days of meditating broken up by the "yogi jobs" they had to do, meals, and sleeping.

The retreat center, aptly called Spirit Rock, was located in the hilly countryside of northern Marin County. There were about a hundred attendees – mostly white baby boomers. Harris was relieved to find he had a single room to himself. His yogi job was pot washing.

After a light dinner, the attendees went to the meditation hall for the opening session. One of the teachers informed them that they had officially entered into silence; there would be no talking, reading, or sex. The goal was for participants to be mindful of everything they did at the retreat – from eating to going to the bathroom. To this effect, they had to carry themselves with exaggerated slowness and pay attention to their every move.

Day Two

On the second day, Harris woke up, took a shower, and followed the others to the meditation hall. He felt uncomfortable when the other meditators stopped to bow to the Buddha statue in the hall. There were lyric sheets at each station in the hall. One teacher explained that yogis have used the chants for centuries as part of their morning routine. He began chanting slowly and the others joined in.

After the chants, the group meditated for an hour. Harris' mind wandered for most of this time – mostly because the cushions he was sitting on were causing him back and neck pain. After meditation, he followed the yogis to the dining hall for breakfast. Everyone looked down. Part of the rules was to avoid eye contact to avoid interrupting the meditative concentration of others.

Harris found it harder to meditate at the center. He speculated he had performance anxiety. Over the period set for walking meditation, he strolled around the center. He had no idea how he was supposed to meditate. In the third meditation sitting, he could hardly focus on his breath. He kept waiting for the bell to ring to signal the end of the session. He felt defeated by the fact that he could not concentrate, even after a year of daily meditation.

After the session, Goldstein explained what walking meditation was not a recess for strolling around. Each meditator was to pick a spot about ten yards long and slowly pace back and forth. The aim was to mindfully note each lifting, moving, and placing of the legs.

As he stood in line with other mute yogis to get lunch, Harris felt lonely and trapped. He felt stupid for using his vacation time at the center instead of going for a vacation with Bianca. As he regained his mindfulness, he reminded himself that it would be over.

Goldstein made another appearance at the dharma talk session to speak about the power of desire. He opined that contemporary culture conditions people to believe that they will be happier if they pursue more pleasant experiences. He asserted that people needed to manage desire with mindfulness and wisdom. Quoting the Buddha, he noted that every moment presents experiences that are, in reality, terrible baits. He emphasized that people have it in them to swim away from the bait.

At the end of the day, the meditators did some more chanting. The metta chant involved sending "loving kindness" to a number of entities, including teachers, parents, and guardian deities.

Day Three

Late morning, Goldstein invited Harris to his office to discuss his progress. Harris remarked that he had some low moments but found reassurance in the knowledge that they would pass. Goldstein told him that that was the essence of meditation.

In the midafternoon session, one of the teachers led the group for metta meditation. The meditators would picture people in their minds and send each of these people well wishes. They would start with themselves and move to friends, neutral people, difficult people, and then to all beings. For each of these people, they wished happiness, safety, health, and a life of ease. The exercise was meant to increase the meditators' capacity for compassion.

Day Four

Being his thirty-ninth birthday, Harris had a feeling it would be his worst birthday. Throughout the meditation sessions, he battled sleepiness and sitting discomfort. He thought meditation should have been easier by now – seeing that everyone else was at ease. His mind wandered to everything the meditation center had stripped away – work, TV, sex, and sleep. He feared he would have to admit he had failed.

Day Five

Harris woke up desperate, doubting if he would last another day at the retreat center. He signed up for an interview with one of the teachers named Spring. Harris confessed that even though he was trying his best, he was getting nowhere with the retreat. Spring explained that he was trying too hard. What he needed was to go with the flow and expect nothing. She said it was a common problem on the first retreat, and that some of other participants were facing the same problem.

In the next sitting, Harris decided to sit and welcome anything that happened. He noted his knee and neck pain, the birds chirping around the center, and the sound of rustling leaves. He focused on each item that came to mind with total ease until it was replaced by something else. He had heard one of the teachers call the practice "choiceless awareness." He was no longer obsessing over this breathing.

Over the next session, he took the same approach and watched his consciousness without trying to direct it elsewhere. It was a new experience, and he found it exhilarating. As he glided from item to item, he came to grasp how fleeting the present moment was and gained a new understanding of impermanence. This experience also gave him insights about his work life, his relationship with others, and his mindless behaviors.

Harris realized that while watching his breath had been tedious and unfruitful, it was a necessary precursor for achieving choiceless awareness. Walking meditation began to click as well. In the metta meditation session, Harris visualized his mother and two-year-old niece. He pictured them in a way he had never pictured them before. The surrealism of the image brought him to tears.

Goldstein gave the dharma talk in the evening session. He explained that Buddha's signature phrase – life is suffering – had been misinterpreted. Buddha meant to say life is unsatisfying, stressful, or unreliable – mostly because it doesn't last. Goldstein noted that people are almost always looking forward to the next pleasant experience. But when you look back, he explained, all the pleasant experiences never lasted.

Goldstein added that the unreliability of life does not mean that one cannot enjoy pleasant experiences. Gaining an understanding of this unreliability can bring one to the realization that no single experience is the source of happiness. Making this realization brings one closer to true happiness – because happiness is self-generated.

As he left the hall, Harris turned towards the Buddha and bowed.

Day Six

Harris woke up feeling more alert than he had ever been. Meditation had become easy, and the world looked magical. He started his meditation session by focusing on his breath. After a period of concentration, he let his mind float to choiceless awareness. He was at peace with everything, and it seemed no bad thing could get to him.

To his disappointment, Harris found that his alertness could not last. He felt sleepy during the afternoon meditation session and had a massive headache afterwards. During the evening session, he felt a rush of restless energy and gave up meditation.

Day Seven

Harris spent the most of the day thinking about when he would leave.

Day Eight

At their scheduled interview, Goldstein informed Harris that the restlessness and change of circumstances he had experienced were part of the journey. It was normal to go from bliss to misery within a short span of time. However, he noted, the fluctuations would lessen with time.

Goldstein ventured out to explain the meaning of enlightenment over the evening dharma session. Part of the process of enlightenment, he explained, was freeing the mind of cravings.

The meditator becomes super-concentrated. In this heightened state of choiceless awareness, things move so fast they are almost blurry.

The meditator feels terror and sublime bliss as his mind takes detours.

The meditator achieves the goal of meditation: he sees that his "self" is an illusion. He sees the nonexistence of his ego.

When the meditator sees through the illusion of "I," he becomes perfected and achieves Nirvana. The self is the source of greed, hatred, and other negative emotions.

Day Nine

In the morning session, Goldstein asked the meditators not to tune out as they approached the end of the retreat. He urged them to resist the urge to think too much about things they had to do once they go back to their worlds. He encouraged them to identify and halt their thoughts of worry by asking, "Is this useful?"

Day Ten

After the morning meditation session, the meditators were allowed to break their silence. The teachers warned them that since they had spent their time at the center in silence, the outside world would seem chaotic.

As Harris binged on TV shows on the plane back home, he realized how fast his old habits had caught up with him.

Key Takeaways

• Every moment presents baiting experiences that only provide a fleeting sense of happiness. Being mindful enables you to understand that you can walk away from these baits and find happiness from within.

CHAPTER 8: 10% HAPPIER

Shortly after Harris got back from the retreat, Westin offered to make him the weekend co-anchor of Good Morning America. In the weeks that followed, negotiations on the new contract stalled over what seemed to be minor issues. Tired of the impasse, the executive producer of GMA called Harris to his office and informed that he would never be the anchor of a major weekday newscast because he neither had the looks nor the voice.

Having gone off the grid for ten days, Harris was bombarded with numerous questions from curious friends and family. His father, who would go on to ask if he had become a Buddhist, told him about a friend who had started meditating and became "totally ineffective." His friends worried that he had joined a cult. When a senior producer at GMA asked about his experience, Harris told her that he meditated because it made him 10 percent happier. He reasoned that 10 percent covered his bases – it did not sound like he was trying to oversell his story, and it represented a good return on investment.

About a month after the retreat, Harris scheduled an interview with Goldstein for his new show on religion called *Beliefs*. Goldstein talked about how he discovered Buddhism while on a Peace Corps mission in Thailand.

"It just seemed so extraordinary to me. Before one is clued in, we're living our lives just basically acting out our conditioning, and acting out our habit patterns, you know... until we look directly at our minds, we don't really know what our lives are about."

When Harris asked Goldstein whether he had achieved enlightenment (cleaned his mind of greed, hatred, and illusions about reality), he said he was still on his way there. He confessed that while he experienced negative emotions, he had learned to let his emotions pass through him without affecting him as much as before.

With his new role as co-anchor of *Good Morning America*, Harris found it challenging to adjust to the content of the show, sitting arrangements, and the natural conversations he was supposed to have with the other co-anchors. On the upside, the show was getting good feedback from the audience. His other shows – *Nightline* and *World News* – also gave him a chance to work on interviews and stories he liked.

Meditation was handy in helping Harris cope with the pressure of his job. He got into the habit of meditating for thirty minutes every day. When work became stressful, he noted how the stress manifested in his body and labeled the physical changes. By practicing the RAIN routine and asking if fussing about an issue was useful, he was able to get back to a productive state.

However, while meditation made him more mindful, it did not completely quiet his chattering mind or help him loosen up on set. When he met Epstein at one of their regular spots, Epstein informed him that meditation would enable him to detach from his emotions but would not necessarily make his anxiety over job performance go away.

Key Takeaways

• Meditation is a way of becoming aware of your mind. In its absence, living is no more than acting out habit patterns.

• Meditation does not dissolve problems. It enables you to handle them better by putting you in control of the response you make to stimuli.

• People go through life getting pushed by "if only" thoughts. The pursuit of the next great experience and the under-appreciation of impermanence is the root of all unhappiness.

CHAPTER 9: THE NEW CAFFEINE

As he attended meditation seminars, Harris learned that scientific interest in meditation was swelling. Most of the studies suggested that mediation had beneficial health effects on subjects with major depression, drug addiction, cancer-related stress, ADHD, and even irritable bowel syndrome. According to one study, mindfulness made workers more focused and led to improved test scores on the GRE.

Studies from as early as 1979 indicated that the gray matter of people who participated in an eight-week meditation course thickened in the brain areas associated with compassion and self-awareness. The same gray matter contracted in areas associated with stress. Another study found that meditators had deactivated the part of their brain that is active when they are lost in thought. The discovery that meditation created a new brain mode challenged the long-standing neuroscientific contention that the brain stopped changing in adulthood. Neuroplasticity, which submitted that the brain changed in response to experiences, replaced this view.

With his new knowledge, Harris was able to get people close to him to reconsider their stance on meditation. His mother, who had been a religious and meditation skeptic, decided to give meditation a try after learning about the findings of the meditation studies. Within a few weeks, she was able to sit for thirty minute sessions – a feat that took Harris a year to achieve. A few months later, she informed Harris that meditation had stopped her snoring.

Harris invited Diane Sawyer to collaborate on a story about the way meditation was inspiring people to try mindfulness in counterintuitive places like General Mills, Procter & Gamble, and Target. He visited the headquarters of General Mills in Minneapolis where the corporate attorney, a woman named Janice Marturano, had convinced the other executives to adopt meditation. For her, it was not the spirituality of meditation that was fascinating. It was the fact that meditation had the potential to make one a better leader and increase creativity and focus.

Marturano extended her understanding of mindfulness to include practical tips. She told Harris that the human brain could not multitask because it had a single processor. When one keeps switching tasks, the brain struggles to get back to where it was – the result being a loss of productivity. She also recommended taking short mindfulness breaks throughout the day. Through these breaks, one could watch his or her breath or note bodily sensations.

As he visited other corporate headquarters to interview executives for the piece, Harris learned that executives were using mindfulness to maintain focus and ensure that negotiations and conflicts did not get out of hand. As meditation gained traction in Silicon Valley, *Wired* magazine opined that for the tech industry, mindfulness was the new caffeine. Harris noted that schools, prisons, and the marines were also adopting meditation.

As meditation caught on, traditionalists like Mark Epstein worried that the mainstreaming of meditation undermined a key Buddhist component: compassion. This view resonated with Harris. Meditation had helped him become calmer and less reactive, but he had ignored compassion, alongside the other Buddhist concepts of karma and reincarnation. Since leaving the retreat, he had not included metta meditation in his daily sessions. He reasoned that boundless compassion was not attainable – at least not for him.

Key Takeaways

• Happiness, impulse control, and resilience are skills that can be acquired by exercising the brain with meditation.

• Meditation not only increases mindfulness but also helps increase focus, lessen stress and depression, and improve leadership capabilities.

CHAPTER 10: THE SELF-INTERESTED CASE FOR NOT BEING A DICK

Harris got a chance to interview the Dalai Lama in the backstage of a conference hall at Emory campus. The Dalai Lama admitted that he occasionally lost his temper. Harris, who always thought the Dalai Lama represented everything he disliked about Buddhism, realized he had harshly misjudged him.

The Dalai Lama gave Harris a new perspective on compassion towards the end of the interview. He asserted that while self-cherishing is natural, being concerned about the welfare of others benefits the self. A study at the Emory campus supported this assertion. When researchers placed subjects in stressful conditions, they found that those who took part in compassion meditation released lower levels of the stress hormone called cortisol. People who participated in volunteer work or performed acts of kindness tended to be happier, healthier, and more successful at work.

Another study found that compassion meditation increased the capacity for empathy and understanding. Research also indicated that compassion was rooted in human nature and had survival benefits. Tribes whose members cooperated and made sacrifices for each other were more likely to win battles against other tribes.

In light of these findings, Harris decided to add metta meditation to his daily sessions. He began these sessions by picturing and sending positive emotions to a benefactor, a dear friend, a neutral person, a difficult person, and all living beings – just as he had learned at the retreat. He had discovered that the aim of this meditation was not to evoke strong emotions but to strengthen the area of the brain associated with compassion. In the months that followed, he realized that being nice had become a daily priority for him.

At times, Harris wondered whether his career was incompatible with his compassion policy. In one such incidence, he was interviewing Paris Hilton when he asked a provoking question that forced her to walk off the set. Hilton's manager and publicist asked the crew not to use the tapes, but the network went on to air the incidence. With the video going viral, one journalist remarked that Harris had been rude.

Key Takeaways

• Metta meditation strengthens the area of the brain associated with compassion and makes the meditator happier, healthier, and more productive.

CHAPTER 11: HIDE THE ZEN

In late 2010, Harris was in India shooting an investigative piece when he learned that Ben Sherwood – who was the executive producer of GMA when Harris had his panic attack – was taking over from David Westin. While they got off to a good start, Harris realized that Westin was a hands-on boss who pored over every detail of the newscasters' work. Harris decided to take a passive approach; he was not going to compete for airtime or go out of his way to make a story memorable.

He realized his strategy had backfired when Westin awarded other correspondents the out-of-country assignments that would have been his. But unlike his former self, he did not call his boss to argue his case. He reasoned it would be uncompassionate to do so because his boss would have to take the assignments from the other correspondents.

Around the same time, Sharon Salzberg, who was a Jew-Bu and a friend of Harris, invited him to a metta meditation retreat in central Massachusetts. In one of the sessions, Salzberg gave a talk on mudita – the Buddhist concept of sympathetic joy. She mentioned that mudita was difficult for most people because they harbored the illusion that another person's achievement should have been theirs.

Back at work, Harris scheduled a meeting with Sherwood and raised concerns that Sherwood no longer viewed him as a major player in the network. Sherwood advised him to pitch more stories, compete for weekday airtime more aggressively, and take a leading role on the cast of weekend GMA. When Harris protested that he did not want to appear bossy, Sherwood, who knew his anchor had become a meditator, told him to stop being so Zen. Harris realized his meditative passivity was compromising his career and making him ineffective, just as his dad had predicted. Instead of letting go when it mattered and working hard, he had resigned himself to a permanently soft approach.

When Harris told Epstein about his meeting with his boss, Epstein advised him to hide the Zen. He noted that the aggressive nature of organizational behavior does not value compassion. People would view him as weak and take advantage of him if he appeared too Zen.

Epstein asserted that it was common for people to misinterpret the dharma to mean they had to be meek or suppress their personal preferences. It was also common to succumb to nihilism and treat everything from an impermanence perspective.

With these insights, Harris decided to up his game. He started taking on every assignment that his bosses proposed, just as he used to do when he was starting out. He got back to finding and pitching stories of interest – something he had neglected for some time. As he got busier, he realized his negative internal monologue was using his fatigue to work through the defenses he had built against it.

When Harris asked how he could strike a balance between ambition and equanimity, Epstein advised him to nurture a healthy nonattachment to results.

"I think for an ambitious person who cares about their career – who wants to create things and be successful – it's natural to be trying really hard. Then the Buddhist thing comes in around the results— because it doesn't always happen the way you think it should."

Still, Harris could not understand how he could devote all his energy to a project and not be attached to the outcome. The trick, Epstein stated, was to give a project the best chance of success and let it have its own life because no outcome is guaranteed. Letting go of uncontrollable variables meant one could to refocus energy on controllable variables. With this approach, failure is not as upsetting at it often is.

Harris realized that this approach (nonattachment to results) is what he always sought since beginning his meditation journey. He made a list of common but often overlooked truths that he had found on the journey.

1. Nurture compassion. You don't have to be a jerk to survive the corporate world. Blind aggression reduces your clarity and effectiveness and costs you some useful allies.

2. Being mindful does not preclude you from competing aggressively.

3. Meditate. It will help you respond – rather than react – to your impulses.

4. Being mindful helps you understand what is worthwhile and what is pointless.

5. Mindfulness does not lessen your creativity. It makes you a better judge of your shortcomings. It brings different thoughts that may make you more creative.

6. Go easy on yourself. Embrace ambiguity.

7. Humility is the antidote of ego.

8. Be firm but kind on yourself. Confront your flaws and forgive your mistakes.

9. Lessen your attachment to results. Obsessing won't change the outcome.

10. Ask what matters most to strike a balance between ambition and equanimity.

END

If you enjoyed this summary, please leave an honest review on Amazon.com!

If you haven't already, we encourage you to purchase a copy of the original book.

63116101R00018

Made in the USA
Middletown, DE
29 January 2018